Eat to Live Diet Cookbook:

Healthy Recipes Collection For Weight Loss, Fat Loss, Flat Belly, Lower Blood Pressure and Higher Energy Levels

By

Brittany Samons

Table of Contents

Introduction 6

Part 1. Sample Main Dishes Recipes 8

    Thai Vegetable Curry 8

    Sweet & Sour Tofu & Veggies 10

    Fat Free Spinach Mushroom Pie 12

    Sloppy Joes 14

    Great Greens 15

    Quick Moroccan Cauliflower Stir-Fry 16

    Broccoli Mushroom Casserole 17

    Pasta-Free Tofu Lasagna 18

    Chinese Apricot Stir Fry 20

    Nuts & Bolts Squash 22

Part 2. Sample Salad Recipes 23

    Russian Fig Dressing 23

    Triple Treat Cabbage Salad 24

    Vegan Ranch Dressing 26

    Broccoli Vinaigrette 27

    Orange Sesame Dressing 28

    Alfredo Sauce 29

    Greens & Berries Salad with Cashew Currant Dressing .. 30

    Mixed Greens and Strawberry Salad 31

    Raspberry Vinaigrette Dressing 33

Part 3. Sample Soup Recipes 34

Quick Corn Stew 34

Tomato Bisque 36

Creamy Butternut Squash 38

Black Forest Cream of Mushroom Soup 39

Part 4. Sample Dessert/Fruit Dishes/Breakfasts 41

Yummy Banana Oat Bars 41

Eat Your Greens Smoothie 43

Cinnamon Fruit Oatmeal 44

Apple Berry-nut Pudding 45

Strawberry Freeze 47

Final Words 48

Thank You Page 49

Eat to Live Diet Cookbook: Healthy Recipes Collection For Weight Loss, Fat Loss, Flat Belly, Lower Blood Pressure and Higher Energy Levels

By Brittany Samons

© Copyright 2015 Brittany Samons

Reproduction or translation of any part of this work beyond that permitted by section 107 or 108 of the 1976 United States Copyright Act without permission of the copyright owner is unlawful. Requests for permission or further information should be addressed to the author.

This publication is designed to provide accurate and authoritative information in regard to the subject matter covered. This work is sold with the understanding that the publisher is not engaged in rendering legal, accounting, or other professional services. If legal advice or other expert assistance is required, the services of a competent professional person should be sought.

First Published, 2015

Printed in the United States of America

Introduction

The Eat to Live diet is a six-week diet meal plan that focuses on optimal health and weight loss. The diet plan promises to help you shed up to 20 pounds within six weeks as long as you consume foods that are high in nutrients and low in calories such fruits, vegetables and legumes, and stringently limit the quantity of dairy, meat and processed foods that you consume on a daily basis.

By following this diet's nutritional plan, you'll finally lose the weight you have tried so hard to whittle away, but more importantly you'll become healthier than you've ever thought you could be. You'll be able to eat till you're satisfied and with great pleasure. You'll feel great & look great.

The Eat to Live diet advances two weight loss plans:

1. An aggressive 6-week vegetarian meal plan for individuals seeking to lose weight quickly.

2. A moderate meal plan that allows consumption of limited amounts of animal products.

The Eat to Live diet includes numerous recipes that can help you lose weight and realize a flat belly because they have ingredients that are potent enough to fight stubborn fat including belly fat. Most of the recipes have greens, onions, beans, berries, seeds, mushrooms and berries (G-BOMS). This book discusses the recipes in detail.

Part 1. Sample Main Dishes Recipes

Thai Vegetable Curry

Ingredients:

4 finely chopped cloves garlic

2 Tbsp. fresh ginger, finely chopped

2 Tbsp. fresh mint, chopped

2 Tbsp. fresh basil, chopped

2 Tbsp. fresh cilantro, chopped

2 cups carrot juice/2 pounds carrots, juiced

1 red, seeded and thinly sliced bell pepper

2 cups green beans (cut in 2 inch pieces)

1 large eggplant, peeled, if desired & cut into 1 inch cubes

3 cups shiitake mushrooms, sliced

1 can drained bamboo shoots

2 Tbsp. Fuhrman's VegiZest/other salt-free seasoning blend, adjusted to taste

1 tsp. curry powder

3 Tbsp. natural chunky peanut butter, unsalted

2 cups divided watercress leaves

1 pound firm tofu, chopped into 1/4 inch thick slices

1/2 cup light coconut milk

1/2 cup raw cashews, chopped

Uncut mint, cilantro or basil leaves, for garnish (if desired)

Directions: Mix garlic, mint, ginger, basil, carrot juice, cilantro, bell pepper, green beans, eggplant, mushrooms, VegiZest, bamboo shoots, curry powder, and one cup of the watercress in a huge skillet. Boil the mixture, cover & simmer, and stir occasionally till all vegetables become tender. Add the peanut butter. Add the tofu, simmer, and toss till hot. Then, add the coconut milk & heat through. Proceed to top this with the cashews and the remaining cup of watercress. If desired, garnish with mint, cilantro leaves or basil. Serve for 8 over quinoa or brown rice.

Sweet & Sour Tofu & Veggies

Ingredients:

1 pound firm tofu

Three Tbsp. fresh lemon juice

Three Tbsp. maple syrup

Three Tbsp. natural style ketchup

1 tsp. dark sesame oil

Three Tbsp. low sodium soy sauce

2 Tbsp. cornstarch

I thinly sliced onion

1 diagonally sliced carrot

Two and a half tsp. shredded ginger root

1 large chopped bell pepper

2 cups sliced cabbage

4 ounces green beans, frozen and thawed or fresh, sliced into pieces

8 ounces of sliced fresh mushrooms

A zucchini chopped into half inch pieces

1 can pineapple chunks in juice, juice reserved

Directions: Squeeze excess water from the tofu and slice it into half inch cubes. Whisk the lemon juice, maple syrup, ketchup, sesame oil, cornstarch and tamari together in a small bowl. Then heat two Tbsp. of water over medium heat in a large skillet or a work or large.

Proceed to add ginger, carrot, and onion and stir till onion becomes translucent. Then add bell pepper, green beans, zucchini, cabbage and mushrooms; cover and steam till tender for about three to five minutes. Add more water if needed. Then, add the tofu, pineapple juice mixture, and pineapple and cook while stirring frequently till the sauce thickens. Spoon the veggies & sauce over the brown rice and serve.

Fat Free Spinach Mushroom Pie

Ingredients:

Dough

1 Tbsp. yeast

Half tsp. salt

3 cups unbleached flour

Half tsp. sugar

A cup of warm water

Filling

1 tsp. salt

1 tsp. oregano

1 cup TVP flakes/granules

7/8 cup boiling water

Half tsp. fennel seeds

1 tsp. basil

2 cups of sliced mushrooms

6 oz. tomato paste

Quarter cup soymilk, brushes top crust

Frozen chopped spinach, thawed & drained

Directions:

Dough: Combine together water, sugar and yeast in a large bowl and let stand for about five minutes. Then, add salt and flour and knead for about five minutes into smooth, elastic dough—kneading can also be done in any food processor with a dough hook—and punch down.

Filling: Combine together boiling water, TVP, salt, basil, oregano, and fennel seeds. Then, sauté this TVP mixture for a few minutes in a large skillet... Afterwards, stir in tomato paste, mushrooms, spinach, and water until heated through.

Preheat your oven to 375 degrees Fahrenheit. Then, roll the dough into one huge oblong shape; spread filling generously on top & roll-up like a jelly-roll. Add a little bit of soy milk to brush top. Bake for thirty to thirty five minutes. If the crust commences to brown as expected, cover with foil during last five to ten minutes. Slice into 16 slices and serve accordingly.

Sloppy Joes

Ingredients:

One medium sized onion, finely sliced

Water to help with sautéing

2 minced garlic cloves

15 oz. (1 can) tomato sauce

Cayenne pepper

1 cup dry TVP granules

Half medium finely chopped Bell pepper

1 tsp. salt to taste

Directions: Sauté bell pepper and onion in about one or two Tbs. of water till almost clear; and then add garlic & sauté for a few minutes. Then, add TVP, salt, tomato sauce and pepper to taste. Reduce heat and simmer for about five minutes or until TVP softens.

Great Greens

Ingredients:

1 bunch Swiss chard with leaves chopped, tough stems removed

1 large bunch kale, leaves dropped, tough stems & center ribs removed

1 minced clove garlic

1 Tbsp. Fuhrman's Spicy Pecan Vinegar/any other flavored vinegar

1/2 Tbsp. Fuhrman's VegiZest/other salt-free seasoning blend, adjusted to taste

1 tsp. dried basil

1 tsp. dill, dried

Black pepper to taste

Directions: Steam Swiss chard and kale together for seven minutes before transferring the steamed mixture to a separate bowl. Proceed to mix the remaining ingredients. Add this mixture to the greens. Add 2-3 Tbsp. of the steaming water for consistency, if desired. Serve for four.

Quick Moroccan Cauliflower Stir-Fry

Ingredients:

1 thinly sliced medium onion

1 cup mushrooms, sliced

2 cups packed kale, sliced

3 cups—approx. 1/2 head—cauliflower, chopped into one inch pieces

1 carton Fuhrman's Moroccan Chickpea Stew

Directions: Boil 2 to 3 Tbsp. of water in a huge sauté pan and water sauté onion for about two minutes. Then, add mushrooms and sauté for one more minute. Proceed to add kale and to sauté till the kale begins wilting. Add cauliflower & Moroccan Chickpea stew. Simmer, cover, reduce heat and cook for about fifteen minutes while stirring occasionally. Serve for two.

Broccoli Mushroom Casserole

Ingredients:

3 cups broccoli florets, fresh or frozen

3 cups brown rice, cooked

8 ounces cleaned and chopped mushrooms

1 1/2 cups kidney beans, cooked/1 salt free drained kidney beans

1 carton (approx. two cups) Fuhrman's Supreme Greens G-BOMS soup

Directions: Preheat your oven to 350 degrees Fahrenheit. Steam fresh broccoli until crisp tender; thaw broccoli if frozen. Then, sauté mushrooms to tenderness and until most of the liquid cooks off. Mix all the ingredients in a two-quart casserole and bake for about twenty minutes or till heated through. Serve for five.

Pasta-Free Tofu Lasagna

Ingredients:

1 minced clove garlic

Two Tbsp. water

4 sliced oz. fresh mushrooms

3 to 4 large zucchini

Dash cayenne pepper

Half tsp. basil

Quarter tsp. basil

1 clove garlic

1 tsp. oregano

1 Tbsp. nutritional yeast

1 jar of spaghetti sauce or favorite sauce

Half pound regular tofu

Half tsp. salt

5 oz. frozen spinach, chopped frozen, thawed and squeezed dry

Soy parmesan, if desired

Directions: Heat water in large non-stick pot, add the minced garlic & cook for sixty seconds. Then, add the mushrooms & sauté them till tender. Add more water if need be. Then, remove from heat and add the spaghetti sauce. Slice all zucchinis into quarter inch slices and steam them in two Tbsp. water about three minutes. Use paper towels to dry them (zucchinis) upon cooling.

Preheat your oven to 375 degrees Fahrenheit. Process the thawed spinach and tofu briefly in a food processor. Then, add rest of the ingredients (except the parmesan & zucchini) to the food processor and blend to smoothness. Spread about half of the sauce in the bottom of an 8 by 8-inch and top it with a layer of zucchini. Spread half of the tofu-mixture on the zucchini. Then, cover with another zucchini layer and pour left sauce over it. Again, top with the final zucchini layer and pour the left sauce over this. Proceed to bake for half an hour. You may sprinkle with soy parmesan if desired.

Chinese Apricot Stir Fry

Ingredients:

two blocks of additional firm tofu, which are cubed in bite-sized pieces

4 Tbsp. water

1 tsp. garlic powder

4 Tbsp. cooking wine

1 tsp. Bragg liquid Aminos

2 Tbsp. Fuhrman's VegiZest

4 Tbsp. apricot preserve –sugar free, 100 percent fruit.

2 to 3 frozen oriental vegetables, mixed and packed

1/2 tsp. Chinese seasoning, salt free

Directions: Put 2 Tbsp. of water in a pan & add the extra firm tofu. Preheat pan at medium heat, and lower the heat once the pan heats up. Drizzle garlic powder over the tofu while turning tofu frequently to prevent sticking. Ultimately, the tofu will release water and you won't need to turn it frequently. Mix the VegiZest, cooking wine, apricot preserves, Braggs Aminos and 2 tbsp. water in a cup. Drizzle half of the mixture over the tofu and continue simmering. Then, steam the frozen vegetables on stovetop or defrost in a microwave. Once defrosted, add vegetables to the tofu. Then, sprinkle the sauce left over tofu-vegetable mix. Add the Chinese seasoning and continue simmering till the liquid largely cooks off.

Nuts & Bolts Squash

Ingredients:

1/2 cup dried apricots

1/4 cup pecans

1/4 cup cashews

1/4 cup raisins

1 Tbsp. Fuhrman's VegiZest

fresh orange juice, minus sugar

2 butternut/acorn squashes

Directions: Cut the apricots, pecans, and cashews into small pieces and mix with VegiZest and raisins. Cover the mixture with enough orange juice. Chop the acorn or butternut squash longitudinally to scoop out seeds. Then, place the dried nut/fruit mixture into the squash's hollow cavity. You may add more orange juice to fill the cavity if you desire. Then, use silver foil to lightly cover the top of each squash half. At 350 degrees, bake in a pan, with 1/3 inch of water in the bottom—water helps maintain moisture. Bake till the squash becomes soft.

Part 2. Sample Salad Recipes

Russian Fig Dressing

Ingredients:

1/3 cup salt free pasta sauce

1/3 cup raw almonds/ 3 Tbsp. raw almond butter

2 Tbsp. sunflower seeds, raw

3 Tbsp. Fuhrman's black Fig Vinegar/balsamic vinegar

1 Tbsp. raisins/dried currants

Directions: Mix all the above ingredients in a powerful blender or food processor and blend until smooth. Serve for two.

Triple Treat Cabbage Salad

Ingredients:

For Salad:

2 cups grated green cabbage

A cup of grated red cabbage

A cup of grated savoy cabbage

1 peeled and grated carrot

1 thinly sliced red pepper

1/4 cup currants, dried

2 Tbsp. pumpkin seeds, raw

2 Tbsp. sunflower seeds, raw

A Tbsp. raw sesame seeds

For Dressing

1/3 cup of hemp, unsweetened soy or almond milk

Half cup of raw cashews/quarter cup of raw cashew butter

one peeled and sliced apple

1 Tbsp. Fuhrman's Spicy Pecan Vinegar/balsamic vinegar

1 Tbsp. currants, dried

1 Tbsp. raw sesame seeds (lightly toasted)*

Directions: Put all the salad ingredients together. Then, blend apple, cashews, non-dairy milk, and vinegar in a powerful blender and toss with salad. Proceed to garnish with lightly toasted sesame seeds and currants. *Lightly toast the sesame seeds in a pan over medium-heat for about four minutes while frequently shaking the pan. This allows for flavors to mix. Serve for four.

Vegan Ranch Dressing

Ingredients:

1/3 cup low fat silken tofu

2/3 cup soy milk

1 teaspoon dried parsley

1 Tbsp. fresh lemon juice

Quarter tsp. salt

Quarter tsp. garlic powder

1 tsp. dried chives

Generously grated black pepper

Directions: Place all the ingredients in a powerful blender and blend till smooth. It makes one cup.

Broccoli Vinaigrette

Ingredients:

1 bulb garlic (separated into unpeeled cloves)

1 large head broccoli

2 Tbsp. Lemon Juice

1 Tbsp nutritional juice

Pinch cayenne pepper

3 dates, pitted

Half cup raw almonds/quarter cup raw almond butter

2/3 cup unsweetened soy (hemp or almond milk)

Directions: Preheat your oven to 350 degrees. Then, roast the unpeeled garlic until soft. Upon cooling, squeeze out the soft cooked garlic while removing and discarding the skins. Blend the garlic with the non-dairy milk dates, almonds, cayenne pepper, nutritional yeast and lemon juice. Cut broccoli into bite-sized florets. Peel stems before slicing them into quarter inch strips. Then, steam stems and florets until they become tender. Toss the steamed broccoli with the desired amount of dressing. Serve for four

Orange Sesame Dressing

Ingredients:

3 Tbsp. unhulled, divided sesame seeds
1/4 cup raw cashew nuts/1/8 cup raw cashew butter
2 peeled navel oranges
Orange juice to regulate consistency
Two Tbsp. Fuhrman's Blood Orange Vinegar/Fuhrman's Riesling Vinegar/white wine

Directions: Begin by toasting the sesame seeds over med-high heat for three min. while stirring with wooden spoon and frequently shaking the pan. Then, mix two Tbsp. of sesame seeds, cashew nuts, oranges, and vinegar in a powerful blender. Add on orange juice to this mix to alter thickness as needed. Drizzle left Tbsp. of sesame seeds on top of the salad. Serve for three.

Alfredo Sauce

Ingredients:

Two cloves garlic
Half cup water
Half cup fat free soy milk
1 tsp. Italian seasoning
Black pepper to taste
1 tsp. vegetarian broth mix such as Bill's Best Chik'nish Seasoning

Directions: In a small saucepan, combine garlic, seasonings, soy milk, water, and broth mix and bring it to a boil. Add the water mixture/cornstarch and stir continuously till thick. It should be served immediately.

Greens & Berries Salad with Cashew Currant Dressing

Ingredients:

Cashew Dressing

1/4 cup raw cashews/Two ounces cashew butter, raw

1/3 cup soy milk

1/4 cup applesauce, unsweetened

2 Tbsp. dried currants/raisins

Salad:

One head romaine lettuce

Five ounces organic baby spinach

1 bag frozen strawberries (defrosted & cut into half)

Directions: To prepare dressing, blend cashew butter or cashews with soy milk & applesauce in a powerful blender till smooth. To the smooth mix, add currants and blend again. Pile the spinach leaves and lettuce on a plate and top with strawberries. Pour juice from strawberries on top of greens. Then, proceed to top dressing over the berries and greens. Serve for 2.

Mixed Greens and Strawberry Salad

Ingredients:

For Salad

One head romaine lettuce

About 5 cups (5 ounces) baby spinach

4 cups fresh or frozen strawberries, sliced and defrosted

For the Dressing:

1/4 cup raw cashews/Two Tbsp. raw cashew butter

1/3 cup unsweetened soy, almond or hemp milk

1 peeled and cored apple

2 Tbsp. currants/raisins, dried

Directions: Begin by piling the spinach leaves and lettuce on a plate toping this with strawberries. To prepare dressing, blend salad ingredients in a powerful blender to smoothness. Then, proceed to top the berries and greens with this dressing. Serve for three.

Note: It is important to use Fuhrman's salad dressings for your weight loss plans because they are a lot of

recipes. Furthermore, the nutritional value of the salad dressings is high because they are raw. They are replete with fiber, low in cholesterol and calories too.

Raspberry Vinaigrette Dressing

Ingredients:

1 Tbsp. chopped shallots

1 Tbsp. Dijon mustard

Three quarter cup unsweetened raspberries, frozen

Quarter cup of raspberry vinegar

Stevia to taste

Directions: Mix all the ingredients properly; or puree until smooth.

Part 3. Sample Soup Recipes

Quick Corn Stew

Ingredients:

One and a half cups water

One and a half cups soy milk

1 Tbsp. whole wheat flour

2 Tbsp. Fuhrman's VegiZest

1 tsp. dulse

Half tsp. Mrs. Dash seasoning

1 tsp. salt free Spike seasoning

1 tsp. date sugar from health food stores

1 tsp. butter buds if desired

1 peeled and diced medium potato

1 diced carrot

1/2 diced medium onion

half chopped medium red bell pepper

1 minced love-garlic

1 bag frozen corn

Directions: Begin by heating soy milk and water together over low heat. Then, mix seasonings, dulse, VegiZest, Butte Buds, date sugar, and flour. Simmer this and add carrots, potatoes, garlic, red bell pepper and onion. Then cover and continue simmering for ten minutes while stirring constantly. Then, being adding the frozen corn till it defrosts and soup boils again. Serve for five.

Tomato Bisque

Ingredients:

3 cups of carrot juice or three pounds of juiced carrots

1 1/2 pounds chopped fresh tomatoes/or 1 BPA-free carton tomatoes, chopped

Quarter cup chopped, salt free, sulfur free tomatoes

Two chopped celery stalks

1 small chopped onion

1 chopped leek

1 large chopped shallot

3 chopped cloves garlic

2 Tbsp. Fuhrman's MatoZest or other salt free seasoning blend

1 tsp. crumbled and dried thyme

One small bay leaf

Half cup raw cashews

Quarter cup fresh basil, chopped

5 ounces spinach/baby kale

Directions: Simmer all ingredients (except the cashews spinach and basil) for half an hour in a large saucepan. Be sure to discard the bay leaf. Then, remove two cups of the vegetables with slotted spoon and set aside.

Blend the left juice with cashews in a powerful blender to smoothness. Then, return the blended soup together with the reserved vegetables to pot. Proceed to stir in the spinach and basil till the spinach wilts. Serve for four.

Creamy Butternut Squash

Ingredients:

Two cups water

Two cups soy milk

1 can vegetable broth, low sodium or salt free

6 hugely sliced carrots

Five organic celery stalks (chopped into half inch pieces)

2 chopped into half onions

Two medium size zucchini (sliced in large slices)

2 peeled and cubed whole butternut squash

3 Tbsp. Fuhrman's VegiZest

One Tbsp. nutmeg

1 tsp. unsalted Spike/Mrs. Dash seasoning

1 tsp. ground cloves

1/2 to one pound cremini, shiitake, and/or oyster mushrooms (with their stems dropped and chopped into half)

Directions: Place all ingredients except mushrooms in a soup pot and boil before simmering for half an hour. Then, blend everything together. Proceed to now add mushrooms and cook for another half an hour.

Black Forest Cream of Mushroom Soup

Ingredients:

2 Tbsp. water

Two pounds of mixed fresh mushrooms—button, cremini, shiitake— sliced 1/4 inch thick

Two minced/pressed cloves garlic

Two tsp. herbes de Provence

Five cups carrot juice or five pounds juiced carrots

3 cups divided, unsweetened hemp/soy/almond milk

2 coarsely chopped carrots

Two medium chopped onions

3/4 cup corn kernels, fresh or frozen

1 cup celery, chopped

3 leeks chopped in half-inch thick rounds

Quarter cup of Fuhrman's VegiZest or any unsalted blend, adjusted to taste

Quarter cup cashews, raw

1 Tbsp. fresh lemon juice

1 Tbsp. fresh thyme, chopped

Two tsp. fresh rosemary, chopped

Three cups cooked white beans—navy northern, cannellini— or two cans salt-free white beans, drained

Five ounces of baby spinach

Quarter cup fresh parsley for garnish, finely chopped

Directions: Begin by boiling the water in a large sized sauté pan. Then, water saute mushrooms, herbes de Provence and garlic for about five minutes or to tenderness. Add more water to prevent sticking if you deem necessary. Put aside. Then, boil the carrot juice, corn, onion, 2 ½ cups of the non-dairy milk, leeks, celery and VegiZest in a huge soup pot. Minimize heat and simmer vegetables to tenderness for about half an hour. Blend the cashews and left half cup of milk in a powerful blender or food processor. Then, to this add the lemon juice, half of the soup liquid & vegetables, rosemary and thyme. Blend till creamy and smooth. Then, return the pureed soup mixture to pot. Proceed to add spinach, beans and sautéed mushrooms before heating until the spinach wilts. Then, garnish with parsley. Serve for five.

Part 4. Sample Dessert/Fruit Dishes/Breakfasts

Yummy Banana Oat Bars

Ingredients:

Two cups quick-cooking rolled oats—not instant

Half cup unsweetened coconut, shredded

Half cup dates or raisins, chopped

Quarter cup walnuts, chopped

Two large mashed ripe bananas

Three-quarter apple, finely chopped

2 Tbsp. ground flax seeds

Directions: Being by preheating your oven to 350 degrees Fahrenheit. Then, thoroughly mix all ingredients in a large bowl. Then, press this into a nine-by-nine inch baking pan & bake for half an hour. Cool on a wire rack and then chop into squares when cool. Serve for eight.

N/B: **For Banana Oat Spice Bars**, add in:

half tsp. ground cinnamon

quarter tsp. allspice

quarter tsp. ground cloves

quarter tsp. ground nutmeg

$1/8^{th}$ tsp. black pepper

Eat Your Greens Smoothie

Ingredients:

Three ounces kale or baby spinach

Two ounces of romaine lettuce

One ripe banana

One cup blueberries, frozen or fresh

Half cup unsweetened soy/hemp/almond milk

Half cup pomegranate juice

One Tbsp. ground flaxseeds

Directions: Simply put all the above ingredients in a powerful blender and blend till smooth and creamy.

Cinnamon Fruit Oatmeal

Ingredients:

A cup of water

One tsp. vanilla extract

Quarter tsp. ground Ceylon cinnamon

Half cup oats, old-fashioned

Half cup blueberries

Two chopped apples

Two Tbsp. walnuts, tablespoons chopped

1 Tbsp. ground flax seeds

Quarter cup raisins

Directions: Combine water, the cinnamon and vanilla in a sizeable saucepan. Then, proceed to boil this mixture over high heat. Then, minimize the heat to a mere simmer before stirring in the oats. When this mixture begins to simmer, proceed to add the blueberries. Then, remove from heat upon berries getting heat all through. Proceed to cover and allow it to stand for fifteen minutes till thick and creamy. Mix in nuts, apples, raisins, and flax seeds. Serve for two.

Apple Berry-nut Pudding

Ingredients:

Two cups apples, dried

1 1/2 cups unsweetened vanilla soy milk

Eight fresh or frozen organic strawberries

Half cup raw Brazil nuts

Half cup raw pecans

One cup of organic baby spinach

Quarter cup of shredded unsweetened coconut

Half Tbsp. cinnamon

Quarter tsp. nutmeg

Six pitted medjool dates

Six fresh organic strawberries—for garnish

unsweetened coconut for garnish, shredded

Directions: Begin by preheating the oven to 300 degrees. Then, soak dried apples in soy milk for at least sixty minutes. If utilizing frozen strawberries, thaw & squeeze water out. Afterwards, combine soy milk, 8 strawberries and soaked apples with remaining ingredients (except for coconut garnishes and strawberry) in a powerful blender and blend to till smooth and creamy. You can add some more soy milk if desired. Then, spoon into small over-proof custard cups or muffin cups and bake for twenty minutes. Proceed to place half strawberry over each pudding cup & sprinkle with coconut. Serve chilled for 12 when chilled.

Strawberry Freeze

Ingredients:

1/3rd cup vanilla soy milk

two ripe frozen bananas

One cup of frozen strawberries

Dash vanilla extract, if desired

1 Tbsp. ground flax seeds if desired.

Directions: Peel and freeze ripe banana in advance in a kitchenware or plastic bag. This ensures that no banana goes to waste—be sure to freeze the ones that begin to get too ripe. Afterwards, place all the ingredients in a powerful blender & blend until creamy and smooth. Serve for two. This freeze is easy to prepare and should only take you five minutes.

Final Words

The Eat to Live Diet has numerous delicious recipes to help you lose weight in a healthy manner without having to skip any meals or stay hungry. As outlined in this book, the recipes are available in various categories i.e. main dishes, salads and dressings, soups, and desserts. Most of them emphasize a strict vegetarian meal plan that can help you achieve rapid weight loss results. When combined with exercise, these recipes can help you whittle 20 plus pounds within six weeks.

Thank You Page

I want to personally thank you for reading my book. I hope you found information in this book useful and I would be very grateful if you could leave your honest review about this book. I certainly want to thank you in advance for doing this.

If you have the time, you can check my other books too.

www.ingramcontent.com/pod-product-compliance
Lightning Source LLC
LaVergne TN
LVHW021741060526
838200LV00052B/3395